Elements of Praise: Poetry of the Spirit

ELEMENTS OF PRAISE:

POETRY OF THE SPIRIT

RITA ROCHELLE BECTON

iUniverse, Inc.
Bloomington

Elements of Praise:
Poetry of the Spirit

Unless otherwise indicated scripture quotations taken from the King James Version of the Bible.

All reference marked NIV scripture taken from the HOLY BIBLE, NEW INTERNATIONAL VERSION, Copyright 1973, 1978,1984 by International Bible Society. Used by permission of Zondervan. All rights reserved.

iUniverse books may be ordered through booksellers or by contacting:

iUniverse
1663 Liberty Drive
Bloomington, IN 47403
www.iuniverse.com
1-800-Authors (1-800-288-4677)

ISBN: 978-1-4502-6258-3 (sc)
ISBN: 978-1-4502-6259-0 (e)

Printed in the United States of America
iUniverse rev. date: 09/06/2011

FOR YOU

JESHUA

Romans 11:16

I've known you most of my life, through good days
and bad. I can testify to three things: one, there is no
righteousness in me; two, You are faithful; and three, You
won't leave. You are the one constant of my life, from now
into the hereafter. My one reality.

*TO YOU BE PRAISE AND GLORY BOTH NOW AND
FOREVERMORE. AMEN!*

"O Lord my God, you are very great; you are clothed with splendor and majesty.
He wraps himself in light as with a garment; he stretches out the heavens like a tent and lays the beams of his upper chambers on their waters.
He makes the clouds his chariot and rides on the wings of the wind."
(Psalms 104:1-3NIV)

CONTENTS

EPILOGUE

ACKNOWLEDGMENTS

I want to acknowledge these people who have poured into my life.

Rev. Clarence Duvall, my first pastor;

The friends who stayed: Anita Jones, Bro Will and Sis Sally, and the Allen Family; also, thanks to

The friends that went away, especially the hidden one for allowing me to repeat the test that failed the first time, and for allowing me to see things from God's perspective.

Rev. Joel Osteen & Rev. Max Lucado for leading me back home.

Chinadeau Ogbuike for reminding me of the gift.

Last, but in no way least, to my family – father and mother, Edward & Brenda (Mommy, thanks for the picture & daddy thank you for being a father); my brothers: Ed, Leonardo & Joe and the rest of my natural family. To my spiritual family Holy Tabernacle COGIC - Pastor Bishop Jack, thank you for giving me a place to grow. Love & blessings to all!

OWED TO A FRIEND

A Memorial: For Angie

WHY DID YOU DIE,

AND I LIVE

WHAT DIFFERENCE DID IT MAKE?

WHY DID HE LAY ME DOWN TO SLEEP

BUT YOU, YOUR SOUL DID TAKE?

WHY DID I GROW

AND LIVE AND LIVE

THROUGH ADVERSITIES EVER DREAR?

BUT THE MEMORY OF YOU

FADED MORE AND MORE THROUGHOUT EACH PASSING YEAR.

WHY DID GOD GIVE ME A FRIEND

TO MEET AND LOVE

TO HELP SHAPE MY WAY?

WHY DID HE LAY ME DOWN TO SLEEP

BUT YOU, HE TOOK AWAY?

WHAT DIFFERENCE DID IT MAKE?

HOW DID HE CHOOSE?

I NOW KNOW IT WAS ALL PART OF HIS PLAN

AND EVEN AT THAT AGE I KNEW

I WOULD EVENTUALLY SEE YOU AGAIN.

WHY CAN'T I REMEMBER YOUR FACE?

OR THE RICHNESS OF YOUR VOICE?

I CAN'T REMEMBER THOSE EARLY DAYS

ONCE I COULD, BUT NOW I HAVE NO CHOICE.

I REMEMBER YOUR NAME

I REMEMBER YOU WERE MY FRIEND, MY FIRST BEST

I KNOW AND UNDERSTOOD THAT

I HAVE NEVER UNDERSTOOD THE REASON FOR YOUR DEATH.

I HAVE ONE MEMORY

IT STAYS WITH ME

I THINK WE OFTEN WENT

TO BUY FRENCH FRIES AT A STAND

WHERE MOST OF OUR ALLOWANCE WAS SPENT.

WE CAN'T ALWAYS SAY GOODBYE

ALL DAYS CAN'T BE FILLED WITH SUNSHINE

NOR ALL MEMORIES BE GOOD.

I CAN'T REMEMBER WHERE WE LAST WENT

OR THE PLACE WHERE WE LAST STOOD.

WHY DIDN'T THEY LET US SAY GOODBYE

WHY DO PARENTS ALWAYS FEAR WHAT THEY CAN'T CONTROL

WHY DIDN'T THEY TELL ME THE TRUTH

INSTEAD OF LETTING IT BE THE NEWSCASTER

WHOSE VOICE WAS ALOOF AND COLD?

I HAVEN'T FORGOTTEN YOU

I JUST CAN'T REMEMBER

EVERY NUANCE, EVERY LAUGH, EVERY SMILE

IT'S LOST SOMEWHERE ALONG WITH

MY LAST DAYS OF BEING A CHILD.

WHY DID YOU DIE

AND I LIVE

WHAT DIFFERENCE DID IT MAKE?

WHY DID GOD LAY ME DOWN TO SLEEP

BUT YOU, YOUR SOUL DID TAKE?

May 28, 2010

AUTHOR'S FOREWORD

One thing I realize as I was writing this book, people today have no recognition of God. They have no general knowledge of Him, or His power, nor do they care. It is unfortunate that people cannot see above this life; they cannot see beyond the everyday hustle and bustle of living. This may be why there is so much hopelessness in the world today.

In the book, on the Contents page I speak of a time before Egypt and then after Egypt. I thought I should explain that. Egypt, for me, was a time when I left God. The thing that caused my fall was a man. A breakup with my ex-fiancé that he got over rather quickly, and showed up with his ex-girlfriend at our church about 3 weeks before we were to be married, and about two weeks after we broke up. I was a young people leader (ages 18-30) of my church and it fell to me to receive in those who had given their life to Christ in that age bracket. His girlfriend joined the church. I thought my Pastor may have a little mercy since he was well aware of everything that had gone on, but he did not. I managed to take her in, but something broke in me then. I think that is when I first cracked. One of my other sisters came up and took over for me, which was a blessing for which I will always be thankful. After service I went over to my best friend's house and cried for hours. I left the church a few weeks later. I visited other churches but I just would sit there and cry—hurting. I felt God allowed me to be humiliated and hurt at home no less, at my church. I felt people were talking about me and judging me. I could not understand why God had allowed this to happen to me. I never asked for money or fame, nope I only asked Him for a family. I remember telling Him, "I know you are God, but you stay away from me and I will stay away from you." I did not want to have anything to do with Him or His church. I felt He had failed me—and that He had used me. I forgot Calvary. I felt He had hurt me and I wanted to hurt Him. Those were some of the darkest days of my life. About a year or so later things got worse. I found out my best friend, the one I mentioned above whose house I went over to and cried that day; the one I had helped lead to Christ; the one who had some children out of wed-lock who I never abandoned. That best friend was marrying my ex-fiancé. That's when in a sense I died. I hated God. I hated men. I hated myself. I had lost hope. The only reason why I did not kill myself during that time was that God prevented me.

In the midst of my rebellion and discouragement God was still parenting me. He is an amazing God. We may not be faithful, but He still is. He will be right there in your mess. I had gotten involved with this guy who I thought was the world, but by the time it was all over, I was praying. I was talking to the Lord regularly. The Lord brought me back to him by using the same thing that drove me away: a man. I did not think I could go back to God, but I started finding Joel Osteen on the television all the time. Soon I started visiting churches and eventually I joined Zion Baptist Church. More than church membership I got alone with God. It was like I was so thirsty for Him, and the more I drank, the thirstier I got. I was happy to be out of Egypt. I was happy to be home.

God had timed it perfectly because I made my way back to Him just over a year before my Mom got sick with the illness that would take her home in 2006. If I were still in the state I was in before, which was drunk most of the time, I would not have been able to care for my mother. Forget handling losing her – that would have done me in. God is gracious like that and He watches out for His children. He strengthens us through every test and prepares us for what is up ahead. He alone is God.

Now back to the test. I left the church in the midst of pain because of what I felt I had lost. I came back and God loved on me; and the people of God loved on me, and all was well. But God is sovereign and He will have His way. So He took me right to where I left. In fact this time – it was worse. After Mom died it started. I got the call to preach. I said yes and the rest is history. Satan started attacking me. When I was drinking and in the world, I had no problems (except the above mentioned man), I had friends, and I was popular at my job. After I said yes to God, literally, all hell broke loose. I bought a house in 2007 (big mistake). In the end of 2007 Dad got diagnosed with cancer. He died in January 2008. The end of 2008 brought about an illness from which I still suffer. The end of 2008 brought the beginning of persecution at my job, and to top it off, the end of 2008 also brought a man.

He was not vain like the other guy, totally different. He was, to me, polite, handsome, easy going, and caring. He was a gentleman and his eyes crinkled in the corners like my Pops. He treated me like I was special. I do not know why I fell for this guy, but I did. For the first time in over five years, I fell in love. I felt it, he did not. In fact, he had a girlfriend. Still, Rita felt God told her that we would marry and spread the gospel together, and despite all common sense, she fell in love. Then the pain started. I felt he was at least a friend. And then he left my life. Without telling me, he just left and that leaving brought everything back. The pain of rejection returned. I had mentioned to a friend that I liked him, you know how that is. I work for public transportation and this one knows that one and so on, so I felt like the whole city was laughing and judging me. This belief extended to the new church I had just joined. Again, I felt like a failure. This time however, instead of running from God, I clung closer to Him. I told Him "As long as I have You, no one else matters." I also started fasting thanks to Jentezen Franklin. During the first 21 days, the writing started. At the end of the 21 days the Lord broke the oppression brought on by the guy leaving. And this time instead of being selfish and internalizing the hurt, I appropriated it the way it should have been the first time. I realized that I had a unique opportunity to see how God felt and to express it. What I mean by this is, everyday God shows His love to everyone, and everyday most people fail to recognize or acknowledge it. This book is the fruit of that realization.

During the process of writing and publishing this book, satan has sought to hinder and abort it through various ways. Among which has been a constant persecution pertaining to the guy I fell in love with. So much so that I almost stopped it's publication. However, I realize that satan does not fight against anything that cannot cause him harm or disrupt his plans, thereby fulfilling the purpose of God. So it is my hope that if this work will save one soul, lifts one spirit, or give someone joy and hope for tomorrow, then this labor has not been in vain.

To me it has been a labor of love, something I can give back to God. The title of this book comes from that intellectual tome to the English language *Elements of Style* by William Strunk, Jr., a book which no matter how I tried, I could not comprehend the complexity of all he rendered. The Bible can be like that. So I thought what I could understand from it, I would share with the hope that you would see Messiah. God is hope. He is happiness and life. That is why I wrote *Elements of Praise*, with the hope that people would take a little time and focus on their God. He is an awesome God. I want people to see and realize that Christ is truly the only reality.

Blessings!

INTRODUCTION

THE OLDER SISTER: BEFORE EYGPT

BEAUTIFUL NATURE

TODAY IS TODAY

TONIGHT IS TONIGHT

TOMORROW'S THE DAY

WHEN THE COLORS ARE BRIGHT

WE WILL THINK OF TOMORROW

WE WILL THINK OF TODAY

WE WILL THINK OF THE FLOWERS SO BRIGHT AND GAY

WE MAY WRITE A SONG

OR A POEM

WE WILL WALK THROUGH THE WILDERNESS

WE WILL WALK THROUGH THE WILD

WE WILL HAVE A SMALL DREAM

A DREAM OF A CHILD

WE WILL THINK OF TOMORROW

WE WILL THINK OF TODAY

WE WILL THINK OF THE FLOWERS

THAT HAVE GONE AWAY

TOMORROW IS TOMORROW

TODAY IS TODAY

(undated 1977 – 1979)

MY MASTER

I have a Master as strange as it seems,

He loves, cares, and watches over me

If I do something wrong,

He will punish me, til He

    makes me see,

    the wrong that I have done;

And if I try to fight,

I know He has already won.

He gave me knowledge so that

    I will be able

    to go to college.

I love my Master;

Don't you love Him, too?

You know He loves, cares and watches over you.

August 8, 1975
9 yrs old

IN SEARCH OF...FRIENDSHIP

The loneliness of the mind,
Body and soul, that takes away
The happiness that is hard to find
And shows you a dark, gloomy day.

To dream of a chance to seek
A new and true life
But you reach a heavenly peak
Only to find strife.

The days go by. The nights pass slow, so
You think your journey will never end,
But you finally figure out the place to go;
There, your journey finished, you find a true Friend.

A Friend that will sort out
All of the strife,
And also give you
Everlasting life.

Undated

WHERE DO I GO FROM HERE?

Where do I go from here?

Will you leave me by myself?

The loneliness and doubt causing me to fear -

Overcoming me and leading me to death.

Where do I go from here?

Do I continue on this road less traveled by?

Or do I wither like a flower before it dies?

Where do I go from here?

Should I check behind me to see if there's direction?

Or should I press and fight my way towards perfection?

Where do I go from here?

The valley is deep; I'm too small to climb,

In this vast universe...

Is this all that is mine?

The pain and confusion,

The starkness of life

Lies, misconceptions, bitterness, strife.

Where do I go from here?!!!!

Lord, thou knowest.

For You are there.

Lead me in Your righteousness,

Protect me from despair,

Hold my hand,

Until You, in Your glory, wondrously appear!

May 31, 1992

THE YOUNGER SISTER: AFTER EYGPT

PUSH

THIS IS TOO HARD!

I SILENTLY SCREAM

I'M SICK OF THESE PEOPLE, THEIR FLESHLY MIND;

AND FEEL ALONE AND ASHAMED

I HANG MY HEAD IN TOTAL DISGUST

SICK OF TRYING, TOO TIRED TO TRUST

'BLESS THE LORD, OH MY SOUL'*

I HEAR THROUGH THE SOUND OF THE RAIN

SO I SHOUT PRAISES TO THE LORD,

FOCUS ON HIM

AND PUSH THROUGH THE PAIN.

June 2, 2010

*Psalms 103:1

I AM

I AM DRAB,

UNCLEAN,

IMPERFECT,

WEAK.

YOU ARE STRONG.

HOLY.

RIGHTEOUS.

BEAUTIFUL.

I AM UGLY,

FAT,

UNSURE,

UNCONFIDENT.

YOU ARE SURE.

OMNIPOTENT.

OMNIPRESENT.

THERE.

I AM LONELY,

IGNORANT,

CONFUSED,

IMPURE.

YOU ARE PERFECTION.

ALPHA.

OMEGA.

WHOLE.

I FEEL YOUR PRESENCE

CLEANSING,

BEAUTIFYING...

I FEEL THY TOUCH.

YOU ARE.

"I AM THAT I AM."*

I AM.

YOUR CHILD.

Undated

*Exodus 3:14

MIGHTY GOD

(Inspired by MIGHTY GOD, sermon by Rev. Charles Spurgeon)

He is the glory

Seated in power

The Priest, the King,

Our refuge & tower

Mighty God!

Scorned by the masses

Beheld by Father

The truth & the life

Our strength with all power

Mighty God!

Undergirding the weak

Guiding the strong

Our rock and salvation

The road that leads home

Mighty God!

Adorned with strength

Israel's & the Gentile's Praise

The four and twenty worship

Continually, Always

Mighty God!

Overcomer, Overtaker,

Irrepressible, Unique

Divine, Holy,

We fall at your feet

Protector, Deliverer

The giver of life

Our designer and redeemer

Our joy in the night

Mighty God!

Majestic in Holiness

Wind walker

Man of war

Shepherd, Teacher, Master & Lord

Mighty God!

Be magnified in the heavens

Throughout the world resound

Ages without end

Be enshrined in Your own power

Mighty God!

Roar through your creation

Your planned domain

Lion of Judah, Prince of Peace

Forever to remain -

Mighty God

Our Lord, Our Master

Our Shepherd, Our Friend

Our Hope, Our Desire

Our expected end

Mighty God

Speak, Messiah, speak

Let your voice be heard

Eternal , Holy

The Only true Word

Seated in the heavens
Proclaimed throughout the earth

Master, Savior

Our only true worth.

Mighty God!

Halle

Halle

lu

jah

November 10, 2009

HAPPY BIRTHDAY, MA

Happy Birthday, Ma.

On your third year in heaven.

I thought it was only two,

I guess it took a year for your death to set in.

I miss you lots,

Our talks and prayers I miss the most.

You probably haven't given it a thought

Being surrounded by the Heavenly Host.

Did it take you awhile to get used to your new place?

Or did you just wander around for awhile

In a stupor,

After beholding His face.

Happy Birthday, Ma

I miss your smile.

I finally put your pictures up

It took me awhile.

Thanks for helping with the passing of Pops.

I know you were there.

Thanks for giving Vinch a break,

God knew what he could bear.

When Pops showed up in heaven,

Was he quiet or was he loud?

It was unnerving how that tall man

Before passing, was as humble as a child.

What's it like in heaven, Ma?

Do your help create the sunsets?

What do you do all day?

I know He took away the cigarettes.

Are you there talking with Michael?

Or conversating with Lot?

Are you joking with David?

Or chuckling with Pops?

Were you surprised when you saw him,

My first, oldest brother?

Was it too good to be true?

You forever a new mother.

What's it like there, Ma?

Is the air clean and pure?

Is the water crisp?

Do the mountains allure?

His kingdom, His place

How is it there?

His abode, His hangout

Our home in the air.

Have you seen my friend Angie?

Does she still look the same?

Did she remember you're my Mom?

Did you remember her name?

How's T.T. and Momma getting along?

I'm sure that after praise and worship

They are talking all day long.

Are Stone and Freeway roaming around?

Her chasing cars,

Stone jumping up and down.

Does the lion really lie down with the lamb?

And who's standing at the gate,

Is it Peter?

Or Abraham?

Have you heard a thousand times,

About the defeat of Goliath?*

Or still absorbing the first hand account

Of the Hebrew boys in the fire?**

Have you seen heavens' entire expanse

Or, are you staring

Mesmerized

At the sea of glass?***

Happy Birthday, Ma.

How are birthdays celebrated in heaven?

Does Jesus, Himself, bake the cake?

I know He can, even without leaven.

How about a cookout?

I'm sure the weather's always fine,

And it is written that our Lord,

Does a mean fish fry.*

Are you birthday folks given a song?

Does Jesus hum the tune?

While the angels sing along?

What other gifts did Jesus reveal to you?

Or will He wait till the whole body

Is gathered there, too.

Happy Birthday, Ma!

Give a shout for me.

Oh, I forgot, I'm already there

As are all who are meant to be.

Singing His praises,

Singing His song,

Lost in His love,

All eternity long.

Happy Birthday, Ma

On your third year in heaven.

I miss you sweet lady,

But I'm learning to accept it.

I'm fine and I'm happy,

And I'm not in gloom.

I miss and love you,

And by His grace,

I will see you soon!

November 14-16, 2009

*I Sam 17   ***Rev 4:5-7
**Dan 3: 8-23   +John 21:9&10

DO YOU REMEMBER?

(Inspired by HAPPY BIRTHDAY, MA)

DO YOU REMEMBER

YOUR ONCE LOFTY PLACE?

DO YOU REMEMBER

THE COUNTENANCE OF HIS FACE?

DO YOUR REMEMBER

THE PLACE OF HIS DWELLING?

DO YOU REMEMBER

WHEN YOU WERE HIS SERVANT?

DO YOU REMEMBER

WHEN YOU GAVE THE CALL TO PRAISE?

DO YOU REMEMBER

CAN YOU RECALL, YOUR HANDS UPRAISED?

DO YOU REMEMBER

THE SOUND OF HIS VOICE?

DO YOU REMEMBER

WHEN YOU WERE HIS CHOICE?

DO YOU REMEMBER

WHEN TIME HAD NO END?

DO YOU REMEMBER

WHEN YOU WERE HIS FRIEND?

DO YOU REMEMBER

FELLOWSHIPING WITH THE ONE?

DO YOU REMEMBER

WHEN YOU WERE A FAVORITE SON?

DO YOU REMEMBER

WHEN YOU WERE VASHTI?*

DO YOU REMEMBER

WHEN YOU WERE ADORNED AS A QUEEN?

DO YOU REMEMBER,

DO YOU HAVE REGRETS?

DO YOU REMEMBER,

OR, HAVE YOU CHOSEN TO FORGET?

DO YOU REMEMBER,

IS IT STILL FRESH IN YOUR MIND?

DO YOU REMEMBER,

YOU ARE CAST OUT FOR ALL TIME?

BUT, 'HAVE YOU NOT KNOWN,

HAVE YOU NOT HEARD',**

I'VE BEEN REDEEMED

THROUGH GOD, THE LIVING WORD.

MY HEART, MY PRAISE,

DO YOU WANT MY LIFE?

NO ACCUSER, NO SATAN,

ESTHER IS NOW THE WIFE.***

THE KING, OUR KING,

TO US HE EXTENDS HIS SCEPTOR WITH FAVOR.+

YOU FELL LIKE LIGHTENING,

BUT WE RISE BY OUR SAVIOR.

DO YOU REMEMBER?

I HOPE THAT YOU DO,

CAUSE ONE DAY VERY SOON

THE KING AND THE KINGDOM

WILL FORGET YOU.

DO YOU REMEMBER?

YOU ACCUSER, YOU LIAR.

DO YOU REMEMBER?

YOU WILL FOREVER BURN WITH FIRE.

DO YOU REMEMBER?

YOU WERE JUST A CREATION FOR PRAISE.

FOREVER REMEMBER,

HE IS 'THE ANCIENT OF DAYS'!++

November 15, 2009

*Esther 1 – 2:4   +Esther 4:11 & 5:1-2
**Isaiah 40:28   ++Daniel 7:9, 13, & 22
***Esther 2:13-17

GREAT WONDER?

WHO ARE YOU,
GREAT WONDER,
WHOM BY YOUR STRENGTH
PUT ALL YOUR ENEMIES UNDER
YOUR FEET?

WHO ARE YOU,
GREAT WONDER,
WHOM BY YOUR STRENGTH
TORE THE VEIL ASUNDER
FOR ME?

WHO ARE YOU,
GREAT WONDER,
WHO BY YOUR STRENGTH
DEATH, HELL AND THE GRAVE YOU PLUNDERED
FOR ALL?

WHO ARE YOU,
GREAT WONDER,
WHO BY YOUR STRENGTH
NATIONS HAVE BEEN CONQUERED
FROM THE FALL?

WHO ARE YOU,
GREAT WONDER,
WHOM BY YOUR STRENGTH
HEM IN THE SHEEP WHO WANDER
FROM YOU?

WHO ARE YOU,
GREAT WONDER,
WHOM BY YOUR STRENGTH
YOU COMPLETELY AND TOTALLY
SUBDUE?

November 17, 2009

UNABASHED AND UNASHAMED

UNABASHED AND UNASHAMED

I HEAR MESSIAH CALLING MY NAME

THROUGH AGES PAST

THE ECHO COMES

MY DAUGHTER YOU CAN MAKE IT

AT CALVARY YOU WON.

UNABASHED AND UNASHAMED

I STAND BEFORE HIM

A PART OF THE CROWD

ON A HILL FAR AWAY

WATCHING MESSIAH SUFFER

TO REDEEM FEET OF CLAY.

UNABASHED AND UNASHAMED

I FALL BEFORE HIM

MY OWN SPIRIT TORTURED AND UPROOTED

TEARS COURSING DOWN MY FACE,

COMFOUNDED,

I'M TOTALLY UNDONE BY THIS DISPLAY OF GRACE.

UNABASHED AND UNASHAMED

I'M STRUCK DUMB

AS I SEE THE RIVETS OF BLOOD

RUNNING FROM HIS BROW

CASCADING FROM HIS HANDS AND FEET

COMPLETELY SOAKING THE GROUND.

UNABASHED AND UNASHAMED

I HEAR HIM CALLING FOR HIS FATHER

THERE ARE WHISPERS AND LAUGHTER

FRIGHTEN VOICES HOWLING

PEOPLE RUNNING TO AND FRO UNAWARE

THE SON OF GOD IS DYING.

UNABASHED AND UNASHAMED

I THINK THIS MUST BE SOME KIND OF DREAM

THIS CAN'T BE REALITY

THE KING OF GLORY

BROKEN, BATTERED, BLEEDING

FOR SIN SICK ME?

UNABASHED AND UNASHAMED

I HEAR MESSIAH CALLING MY NAME

I RUN, I FALL, I HEAR, I CALL

I STAND, I RUN, I FALL, I SEE.

STILL I HEAR HIM CALLING ME

SO HERE I STAND

UNABASHED AND UNASHAMED.

November 26, 2009

WHAT SAYEST THOU, KING OF JACOB?*

(Inspired by I AM JESUS: TO WHOM WILL YOU LIKEN ME?
before completion)

WHAT SAYEST THOU, KING OF JACOB?

DO YOU CONSIDER OUR FATE?

WHAT ARE YOU THINKING, HOLY REDEEMER?

WHAT PROMISES SHOULD WE MAKE?

WHAT SAYEST THOU, KING OF JACOB?

WHY DO WE STAND AFAR OFF?

PLEASE DRAW CLOSE TO US

AND KEEP US FROM BEING LOST.

WHAT SAYEST THOU, KING OF JACOB?

WHAT SPEAKEST THOU TODAY?

HELP HUMAN EARS HEAR YOUR WORDS-

HELP US HEAR EVERYTHING YOU SAY.

WHAT SAYEST THOU, KING OF JACOB?

FRIEND OF ABRAHAM,

LEADER OF YOUR PEOPLE ISRAEL,

FATHER OF EVERY MAN.

WHAT SAYEST THOU, KING OF JACOB?

WHY IS IT HARD FOR US TO HEAR?

WHY DO WE HIDE OUR FACE FROM YOU?

WHY DO WE FEAR?

WHAT SAYEST THOU, KING OF JACOB?

WHAT NEW THING WILL YOU REVEAL,

TO HELP ALL TO SEE YOUR LOVE EXPRESSED

UP ON CALVARY'S HILL?

WHAT SAYEST THOU, KING OF JACOB?

WHY DO YOU CONSIDER US?

HOW DID YOU FALL IN LOVE,

WITH JUST PARTICLES OF DUST?

WHAT SAYEST THOU, KING OF JACOB?

SPEAKEST PLAIN AND TRUE,

LET YOUR WORDS BE SWEET TO US,

LET THEM DROP LIKE THE FRESH MORNING DEW.

WHAT SAYEST THOU, KING OF JACOB?

WHY DO YOU CARE SO MUCH?

WHEN YOUR SHEEP GET DISTRACTED

AND START TO TRUST IN LUCK.

WHAT SAYEST THOU, KING OF JACOB?

MAKE US STILL SO WE WILL ABSORB

EVERY SINGLE ENUNCIATION

OF OUR HOLY LORD.

WHAT SAYEST THOU, KING OF JACOB?

YOU LOVE US THROUGH AND THROUGH.

YOU LOVE US WHEN WE MISS THE MARK,

AND YOU LOVE US WHEN WE'RE TRUE.

YOU LOVE US FOR SOMETHING WE'RE NOT,

YOU LOVE US HERE AND NOW

YOU LOVE US FOREVER AND EVER

AND WE'LL NEVER UNDERSTAND HOW?

WHAT SAYEST THOU, KING OF JACOB?

OUR HEARTS BELONG TO YOU.

DO I HEAR YOU DECLARE,

*"BEHOLD, I MAKE ALL THINGS NEW!"***

November 30, 2009

*Isaiah 41:21   **Rev 21:5 (NKJV)

AGAPE

(Inspired by WHAT SAYEST THOU KING OF JACOB?)

I LOVE YOU WHEN YOU ARE RIGHT

I LOVE YOU WHEN YOU ARE WRONG

I LOVE YOU WHEN YOU DECIDE

THAT IT'S TO ME YOU BELONG.

I LOVE YOU WHEN YOU ARE HAPPY

I LOVE YOU WHEN YOU ARE MAD

IT CRACKS ME UP TO SEE YOU

LIKE A BABY ACTING LIKE YOU SO BAD.

I LOVE YOU WHEN YOU SMILE

I LOVE YOU WHEN YOU LAUGH

I LOVE YOU WHEN YOU ATTEND

SUNDAY SERVICE OR, HOLY MASS.

I LOVE YOU WHEN YOU RUN

I LOVE YOU WHEN YOU WALK

I ESPECIALLY LOVE YOU WHEN IT 'S TO ME

YOU INCESSIVELY TALK.

I LOVE YOU WHEN YOU SLEEP

I LOVE YOU WHEN YOU AWAKE

I LOVE EACH AND EVERY ONE

OF THE BREATHS THAT YOU TAKE.

I LOVE YOU WHEN YOU REMEMBER ME

I LOVE YOU WHEN YOU FORGET

I LOVE YOU WITHOUT RHYME OR REASON

I LOVED YOU BEFORE YOU WERE YET.*

I LOVE YOU FOR NO REASON

I LOVE YOU FOR EVERYTHING

I LOVE YOU WHEN YOU PRAISE

AND WORSHIP ME AS YOUR TRUE KING.

I LOVE YOU FOR TOMORROW

I LOVE YOU FOR TODAY

I LOVE YOU IN SO MANY

UNIQUE AND WONDERFUL WAYS.

I LOVE YOU FOR A MOMENT

I LOVE YOU FOR TODAY

I LOVE YOU FOR A MONTH – A YEAR,

I LOVE YOU FOR ALWAYS.

I LOVE YOU FOR EVERY

WONDERFUL BEAT OF YOUR HEART

I LOVE THAT YOU HAVE BELIEVED IN ME

SO WE WILL NEVER BE APART.

I LOVE WHEN YOU ANSWER ME

I LOVE YOU WHEN YOU CALL

I LOVE YOU WHEN YOU REALIZE

THE GRAND PLAN I HAVE FOR ALL.

I LOVE YOU WHEN YOU WIN

I LOVE YOU WHEN YOU LOSE

I LOVE YOU WHEN YOU REALIZE

I WILL MOVE WHEN I WILL MOVE.

I LOVE YOU WHEN YOU FALL

I LOVE YOU WHEN YOU STAND

I LOVE YOU WHEN YOU COME TO ME

AND TALK MAN TO GODMAN.

I LOVE YOU WHEN YOU PRAY

I LOVE YOU WHEN YOU SING

I LOVE YOU WHEN YOU REALIZE

I CAN DO ANYTHING.

I LOVE YOU, OH, I LOVE YOU

I DO, I DO, I DO.

THAT'S WHY YOUR HEART MAKES THE SOUND

LOVE YOU, LOVE YOU, LOVE YOU.

November 30, 2009

*Jer 1:5

SEE ME IN THE SPIRIT: THE VOICE OF JESUS

See Me in the fire

See Me in the rain

See Me beyond your human

Capacity to explain.

See Me before Pilate

See Me among my brothers

See Me stand in silence

Not one word will I utter.

See Me, My face streaming drops of blood

See Me, the Holy One dying

To place you above.

Now, See Me beyond your pain

Degradation and despair

Beyond life's hope & failures,

& grandeur.

See Me beyond the struggle

Hindrances & snares;

Beyond life's pitfalls and shame

& burdens to bear.

See Me in the fire

Ever consuming and growing

In the fire dancing, shaping,

& molding.

See Me in every dream

Every imparting and foretelling,

Showing.

See Me in the temple

The lamb pure and clean

Now through the Spirit in the temple of you –

ruling and deciding,

Reigning.

See Me in every cloud

Every expanse of heaven

See Me in the rain

Mercy poured out like leaven.

See Me in the smile

On every single face

See within Me mercy & grace.

Close your eyes and look...

See Me in the fire!

See Me in the rain!

See Me in the smile!

See Me in the pain!

See Me in the dream!

See Me in the struggle!

See Me in the temple!

See Me in the molding!

See Me on the cross!

See Me in your heart!

Before you can begin

You must see Me.

God and man

One and the same

Complete and pure

Holy and secure.

See Me… look for Me &

You will find Me

Knock and the door will open

Speak and it will come to pass

Proclaim and it will preach

'Let there be…..'

'Let there be….'

'Let there be….'*

A wife falls in a garden**

God kicks her out***

God walks into a latter garden+

And with His bride in His heart He walks out.++

See Me!!!

"...come, I will show you the bride, the Lamb's wife. And he carried me away in the Spirit...and showed me the great city, the holy Jerusalem..." Rev 21:9b&10 (NKJV)

*Gens 1:3   **Garden of Eden   ***Gens 3:6-24
+Gethsemane   ++ Headed for Calvary

TRIUNE GOD AS ONE

(Inspired by sermons 'Season of the Father' & 'Season of the Son' by Bishop Jack, Pastor – Holy Tabernacle COGIC)

SEASON OF THE FATHER

CREATED BY THE SON

ACTIVATED BY THE SPIRIT

TRIUNE GOD AS ONE

SEASON OF THE FATHER

SIRED BY THE SON

BIRTHED BY THE SPIRIT

TRIUNE GOD AS ONE

SEASON OF THE FATHER

BLESSINGS FOR EVERMORE

SENT DOWN FROM HEAVEN

NOW STANDING AT YOUR DOOR

SEASON OF THE FATHER

HIS GREAT LOVE ON DISPLAY

HIS VISION OF HIS PEOPLE

BEHOLD, THE SLEEPING BABE

SEASON OF THE FATHER

PRODUCED BY THE SON

DELIVERED BY THE HOLY SPIRIT

CHRISTMASTIME HAS COME

SEASON OF THE SON

TO REDEEM FROM THE LAW

TO SAVED BY HIS SPIRIT

TO BE SAVIOR OF ALL

SEASON OF THE SON

GOD'S INFILTRATION COMPLETE

HIDDEN IN A MANGER

A PLAN SO UNIQUE

SEASON OF THE SON

GOD'S PLAN REVEALED

REDEMPTION IN A CRIB

THE WRITTEN WORD IN FLESH CONCEALED

SEASON OF THE SON

THE PROMISE FULFILLED

HOPE LIVING AMONG US

THE SERPENT'S HEAD TO KILL*

SEASON OF THE SON

THE ADAM PERFECTED

THE CHURCH INCORPORATE

DEFEAT IS REJECTED

SEASON OF THE SPIRIT

BREATHING LIFE INTO LIFE

RAISING THE SON FROM THE DEAD

SO ALL CAN HAVE ETERNAL LIFE

SEASON OF THE SPIRIT

THE BABE** NOW PHYSICALLY ALONE

FAITH MEETS BELIEF

GOD'S POWER IN MAN IS SHOWN

SEASON OF THE SPIRIT

NOW THE TIME HAS COME

FOR ALL TO WALK IN VICTORY

AND GET GOD'S WORK DONE

SEASON OF THE SPIRIT,

CHRIST'S BREATH AND LIFE,

EVER INCREASING IN KNOWLEDGE

GENTLY PREPARING HIS WIFE***

SEASON OF THE SPIRIT

ACCOMPLISHED BY THE SON

PURPOSED BY THE FATHER

TRIUNE GOD AND CHURCH AS ONE!

Completed May 2010

*Gens 3:15

** The Early Church After Christ's Ascension

*** The Latter Church Incorporate

SPIRIT OF FIRE

Spirit of fire,

   Spirit of praise

      Don't stand aloof

         Shock, thrill and amaze

            Your people, Your glory

               To perpetrate Your story.

Shine forth O Transcendent One

   Breathe life into death

      Overshadow Your people

      Cause us to be blessed

         Delight us with Your passion

         Fill us with Your desire

Let our lips speak forth Your praise

   And our bodies fulfill Your desire

      Roam thru the depths of our hearts

      Clean each crevice and thought

         Build Your kingdom 'on earth as it is in heaven'+

            Let our bodies be acceptable for you to dwell in

            Cause us to ride above the earth

            Cause us to have eternal, new birth

Spirit of fire

Spirit of passion

Shape us,

Mold us,

Completely fashion

Your church, Your body.

Make us whole

Make us clean

Wash us white

Let us live again

Enter dear Spirit

Control of us completely assume

Till we become flames of fire

Who like our God burns, but is not consumed++

Burn thru and in us

Our flesh and carnality continue to subdue

Fulfill your desire to love and to save

Until we are reflections of Your fire

A glorious and acceptable offering for You!!!

May 12, 2010

+Matthew 6:10 ++Exodus 3:2

I AM JESUS: TO WHOM WILL YOU LIKEN ME?*

(Inspired by Isaiah 40)

TO WHOM THEN WILL YOU LIKEN ME?

TO WHOM WILL YOU COMPARE?

I AM THE GOD WHO IS ALWAYS PRESENT

I AM THE GOD OF EVERYWHERE

I OVERCOME EVERY OBSTACLE

MY EYE IS ON EVERY SPARROW

MY EYE BEHOLDS EVERY SPECTACLE

TO WHOM THEN WILL YOU LIKEN ME?

TO WHOM WILL YOU COMPARE?

I AM THE GOD WHO IS ALL POWERFUL

LET ALL MY FOES BEWARE

I MAKE RIVERS IN THE DESERTS

I MAKE ROADS IN THE WILDERNESS**

I PROVIDE AND PROTECT MY PEOPLE

I'M THE REASON WHY THEY ARE BLESSED

TO WHOM THEN WILL YOU LIKEN ME?

TO WHOM WILL YOU COMPARE?

I AM THE GOD WHO KNOWS ALL THINGS

MY KNOWLEDGE WITH YOU I SHARE

THERE'S NOTHING MADE THAT I DID NOT MAKE***

AIRPLANES, COMPUTERS, BOOKS,

ALL THINGS EXISTS BECAUSE OF ME

AND YET, YOU WILL NOT GIVE ME A SECOND LOOK?

TO WHOM THEN WILL YOU LIKEN ME?

TO WHOM WILL YOU COMPARE?

I AM THE GOD OF BROKEN DREAMS

I AM THE GOD WHO CRUSHES DESPAIR

I HAVE PLANTED EVERY GOOD FRUIT

I HEAPED OCEANS WITH CREATURES OF EVERY KIND

I HAVE CATTLE ON A THOUSAND HILLS+

I HAVE SHAPED AND PLANNED FOR WHAT IS MINE

I AM THE GOD OF ABRAHAM++

YOUR FATHER OF THE FAITH

I AM THE GOD OF DAVID

MY KING OF WAR AND GRACE

I AM THE GOD OF RAHAB

IN MY HUMAN LINEAGE IS SHE

I AM THE GOD OF YOU

IF YOU WILL LET ME BE

TO WHOM THEN WILL YOU LIKEN ME?

TO WHOM WILL YOU COMPARE?

CONSIDER ALL THESE THINGS

AND OF ME BECOME AWARE

I AM GOD, THE LORD

THERE IS NO ONE ELSE.

NO OTHER SAVIOR

BESIDES MYSELF!+++

May 27, 2010

*Isaiah 40:18
**Isaiah 43:19
***Romans 11:36
+Psalms 50:10
++Gens 26:24; 28:13; Ex 3:6; 15, 16; I KI 18:36; Mat 22:32;
    Mk 12:26; Acts 7:32
+++Isaiah 43:10b & 11

IRREPRESSIBLE CHRIST

(Inspired by John 12:19)

Get ready, get set

For the love of your life

The One, the Only

The Irrepressible Christ

Creator of everything

Hindered by none

Perceive ye prevail nothing*

The Jewish leaders wanted to know

They wanted to stop Him

But He continued to grow

The Master - The Teacher

The One who created it all

Dodged and alluded them as

They tried to make Him fall

'Tell us good Teacher'**

They subtlety queried

To whom to pay taxes?'***

'What is the greatest commandment?'+

Then they sought to contradict what they heard

Not realizing – not knowing

That He was the true Word

The fulfillment of prophecy

They had a chance to see destiny

But they were totally blinded

To 'righteous' to see it

The God who was man

Fulfilled all the law in His service

The Sabbath for man

Not the man for the Sabbath++

He focused on,

And enveloped His purpose

Calvary was His goal

The place He would save us

On He went forth

Spreading the gospel for proof

Demonstrating His love

While from the prince of this world He grew more aloof

He never turned away

He set His face like a flint

And carried a world to save

To Calvary – to death

He willingly went

Completing His journey

The reason He was sent

Now Let Him live in you

And you continue to dwell in

The place of joy

This place beside Him

You, His hidden glory

You, the continuation of His story.

So get ready, get set

For the love of your life.

The One. The Only.

The Irrepressible Christ!

Completed May 31, 2010

*John 12:19
**Mat 19:16, Mk 10:17, Lk 18:18
***Ma 22:17, Mk 12:14, Lk 20:22
+Mat 22:36
++Mk 2:27

PRICELESS ONE

Treasure of heaven

Glory of all the earth

Who can measure

Your true worth?

Creation's Crown

Heaven's Weight

Man's true joy

All should celebrate

Giver of life

Chief Architect

Perfect Planner

Defender of the defenseless

The great I Am

Helper of the helpless

Blessing of all

Man's Defender

Bread of heaven

The only One who satisfies

Burden Bearer.

The Truth to every lie

The One Who alone shines

Brighter than the sun

Our perfect Redeemer

The Priceless One.

May 31, 2010

BLESSED HOPE

'Death thou shalt die'*

The poet calls.

Yet in the street

And in the heart

Another falls.

The grip of Hades

Binds the life

Dragging it into the darkest night.

From the first garden to Calvary's hill

Day after day

Till the Priceless One bowed

His glorious head;

And instead of being enveloped

He enveloped death and made it His own

To cause His people to forget

Its fear – its hold;

And call them forth to peace

And a bright, everlasting home.

Breaking sin's bond

Setting us free

Taking us to the place

Where we were meant to be

When your time comes close your eyes

let your fears elope

lift your soul to heaven

And praise The Blessed Hope

May 31, 2010

*John Donne, *"Death Be Not Proud"*

ISHI
(MY HUSBAND)*

Speak Ishi, Speak
let Your voice be heard
set the captives free
cause them to know Your Word
Betroth us to Your precious side
all our pain, fear and sin hide
Cover under the shadow of your wings
Great Eagle, Lofty One,** protect us from everything.

Breath Ishi, breath
Your life into us
How do You to us - Your heart entrust?
Teach us to love You
in spirit and in truth***
Help us to have and to hold
Your church as You
Complete us in our imperfection
Help us to yield to Your correction.

Live Ishi, live
Your life through us
Cause us to hear and move without doubt or mistrust
To be Your eyes, hands, and body
That the spiritually dead may finally see
What life is like
For those who have You, for glorious eternity!

May 31, 2010

*Hosea 2:16
**Isaiah 57:15
***John 4:23

EPILOGUE

ELEMENTS OF PRAISE

THE KEY TO THE HEART OF THE ANCIENT OF DAYS:

FANS FLAPPING

FEET STOMPING

FACES SHINING BRIGHT

MUSIC CASCADING

FEARS FADING

WAVE OFFERINGS BEING OFFERED UP

HEARTS ABLAZED

THE SPIRIT RAISED

TO FIX ALL THAT IS WRONG

UNITY

DIVINITY

PEACE SURPASSING UNDERSTANDING

THIS IS THE KEY TO ONENESS WITH GOD:

ALL ACKNOWLEDGING

AND RECOMMENDING

THE KING OF KINGS

THE LORD OF HOSTS

HOLY IS HIS NAME

THE FIRE

THE HEART

THE EVIDENCE OF

JESUS CHRIST,

THE LION OF JUDAH,

OUR CENTRAL ELEMENT OF PRAISE!!!

FOR EVER... AND EVER... AND EVER. AMEN!

June 2, 2010

"...My soul glorifies the Lord and my spirit rejoices in God my Savior,"
(St. Luke 1:46 – 47 NIV)